SCALE SHA

GRADE 5

for piano

Based on the requirements for Grade 5 of
the Associated Board of the Royal Schools of Music

Using the Stocken Method

This book © Copyright 2008 Chester Music
Order No. CH74701
ISBN 978-1-84772-831-9
Cover and template design by Phil Gambrill.
Printed in the EU.

CHESTER MUSIC
part of The Music Sales Group
14-15 Berners Street, London W1T 3LJ

by
FREDERICK
STOCKEN

This series of books shows Scale Shapes using the Stocken Method and is based on the technical exercises required by the piano grades of the Associated Board of the Royal Schools of Music. In fact this grade 5 book contains all major and minor scales and arpeggios. Even without the goal of an examination, the scales chosen by the Associated Board provide carefully thought-out exercises at eight levels which provide an excellent basis for daily study. It is hoped that the principles established here will soon be extended to other compilations of scales including jazz scales.

I always loved playing scales and other technical exercises as a child – and still do. However, when I came to teach the piano and organ I quickly discovered that many students, especially children, find them to be drudgery. Although the repetitive nature of the exercises is often cited as the main cause of boredom, I believe that this is not often in reality the root of the problem. The student who complains of the tedium of repetition when practising scales might well be the same person who has a fitness programme that involves plenty of repetition and which is found to be most enjoyable.

The mental block many students have with practising scales is not the repetitiveness as such, but the actual technical difficulties involved in reading musical notation and translating this into the physical shapes of the scales themselves. It is these difficulties that seem to prevent the satisfying rhythm of repetition and growing control that the student might find so rewarding when lifting weights or practising kicking a ball into a net.

The method I have invented provides a system which allows the student to concentrate exclusively on the physical shapes of the technical exercise and, in consequence, to focus on the acquisition of good legato, even fingers, firm tone and a musical contour. In short, I have found that this method helps to make scales become fun.

The Stocken Method is not designed to be a substitute for the acquisition of the ability to read staff notation. *In fact the opposite is the case.* I have found that using this method, which so explicitly presents the physical shapes of different keys at the keyboard, actually helps fix these shapes in the student's mind so that playing from musical notation in the context of a piece or sight-reading actually becomes easier.

However idealistic a teacher may be that a student will learn a scale or technical exercise from staff notation, experience shows that the simplest method of introducing a new scale or other technical exercise is often for the teacher physically to play the exercise demonstrating the new shape for the student to copy. The Stocken Method not only removes this stage of teaching, saving valuable time during lessons, but also gives the student a system for the exercise that he or she will be confident of being able to re-read when the teacher has gone.

At the earlier stages of learning, a simple scale may involve ledger lines or other symbols that are far in advance of the pieces a student may be playing. This is the case right from the beginning when the introduction of a C major scale of two octaves, for instance, will use a great many more notes in different octaves than the student will have encountered in staff notation. Many students at much higher levels continue to find key signatures and other aspects of staff notation confusing and find the simplicity of this method to be of great help.

In fact, one of the revolutionary aspects of the Stocken Method is that the complications of staff notation are no longer linked to the often quite different physical complications of actually playing a given scale. This means that scales which have, until now, seemed more difficult than others, mainly because of the complexity of their representation using staff notation, are now, using this method, suddenly found to be easier. The implication of this for the order in which scales have traditionally been introduced to the student is far-reaching.

Frederick Stocken.

SCALES AND ARPEGGIOS

Scales (similar motion)
    all keys major and minor   hands together *and* separately   3 octaves
    (minors melodic *or* harmonic at
      candidate's choice)

Contrary-motion scales
    Group 1: F, D♭/C♯ majors and *harmonic* minors   hands beginning on the key-note (unison)   2 octaves
or Group 2: F♯, B♭ majors and *harmonic* minors

Chromatic scales
    beginning on any note named by the examiner   hands together *and* separately   3 octaves

Chromatic contrary-motion scales
    beginning on D (unison) and on A♭ (unison)   2 octaves

Arpeggios
    all keys, major and minor   hands together *and* separately   3 octaves

Contents

Contents

With minor scales, candidates choose melodic or harmonic

C MAJOR SCALE

Hands separately and together an octave apart in similar motion: 3 Octaves, up and down.

♩ = 63 *(minimum speed recommended by the ABRSM)*

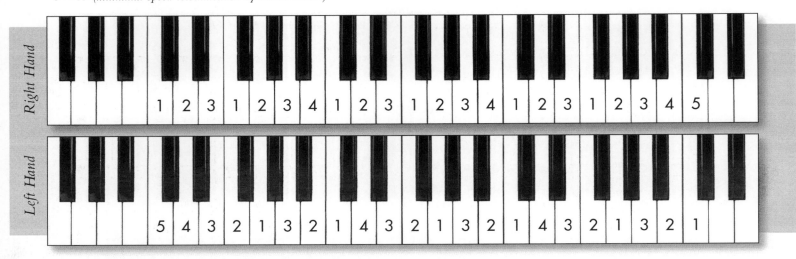

C MINOR HARMONIC SCALE

Hands separately and together an octave apart in similar motion: 3 Octaves, up and down.

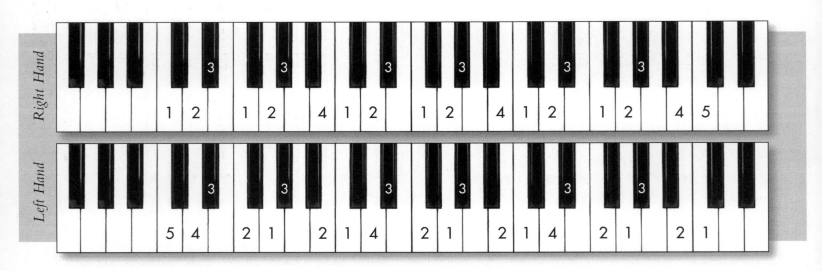

N.B. The scales (including contrary motion and chromatic) are written without a time signature in groups of four quavers with the final note as a crotchet.

C MINOR MELODIC SCALE

Hands separately and together an octave apart in similar motion: 3 Octaves.

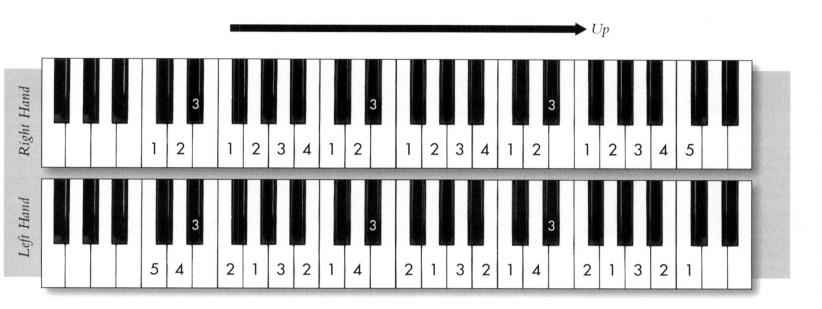

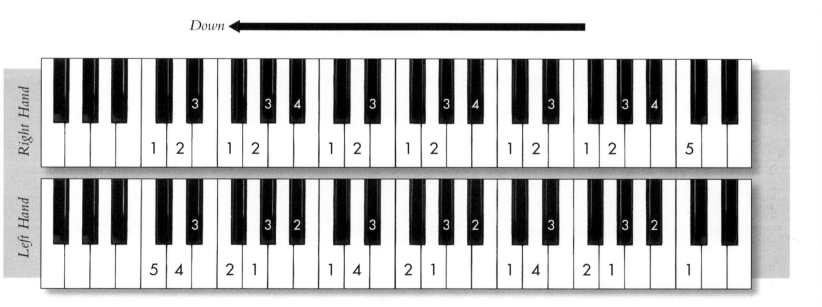

G MAJOR SCALE

Hands separately and together an octave apart in similar motion: 3 Octaves, up and down.

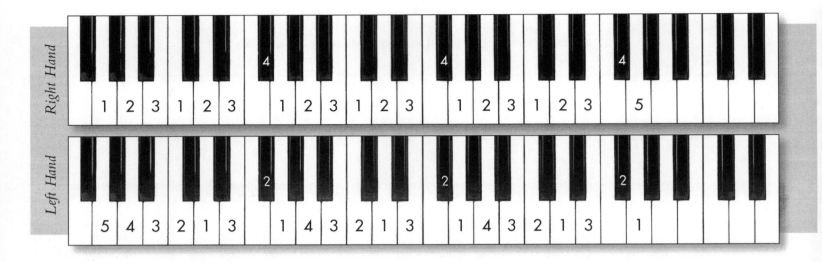

G MINOR HARMONIC SCALE

Hands separately and together an octave apart in similar motion: 3 Octaves, up and down.

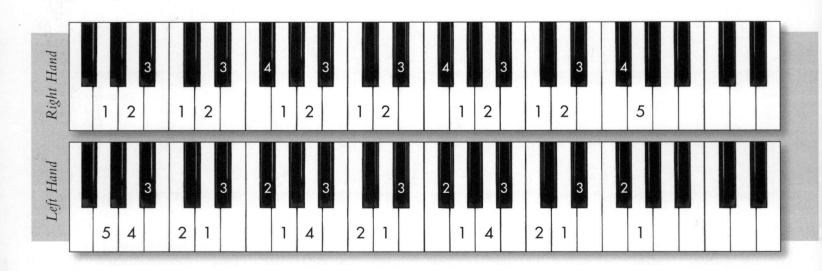

G MINOR MELODIC SCALE
Hands separately and together an octave apart in similar motion: 3 Octaves.

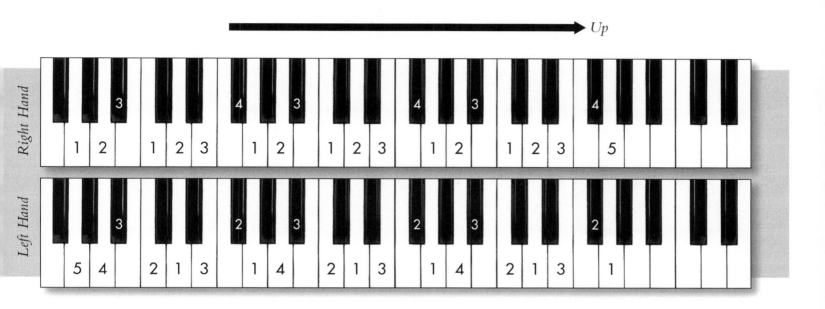

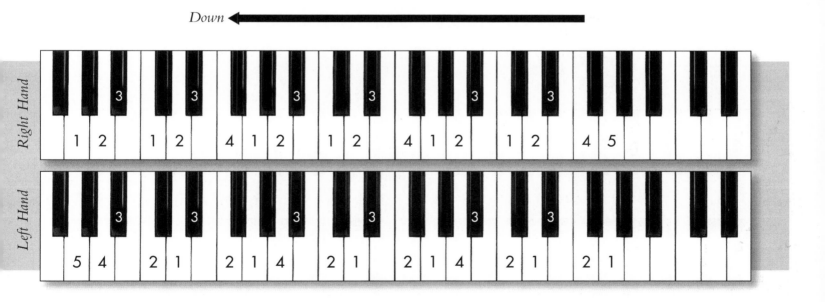

D MAJOR SCALE

Hands separately and together an octave apart in similar motion: 3 Octaves, up and down.

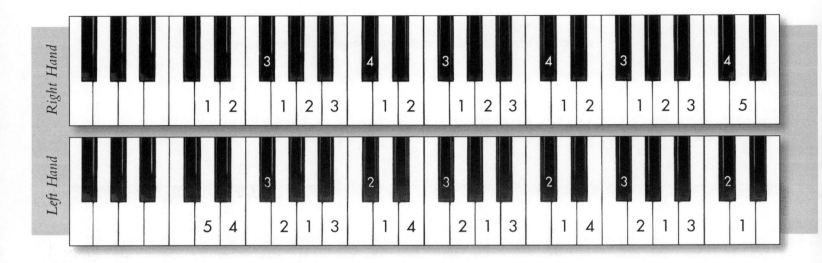

D MINOR HARMONIC SCALE

Hands separately and together an octave apart in similar motion: 3 Octaves, up and down.

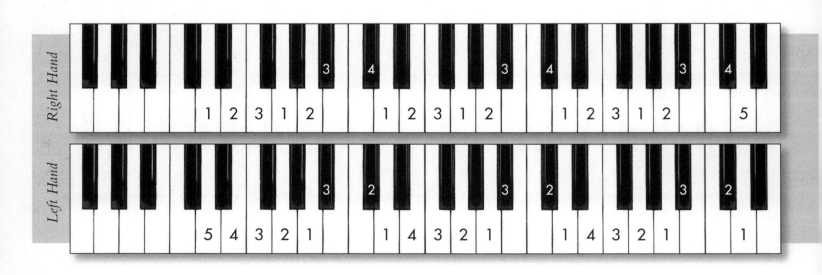

D MINOR MELODIC SCALE

Hands separately and together an octave apart in similar motion: 3 Octaves.

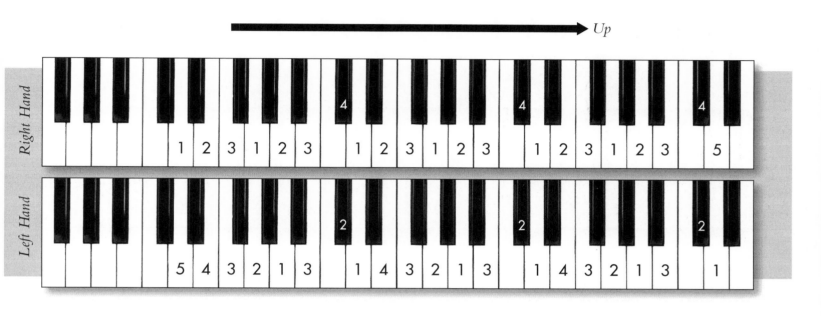

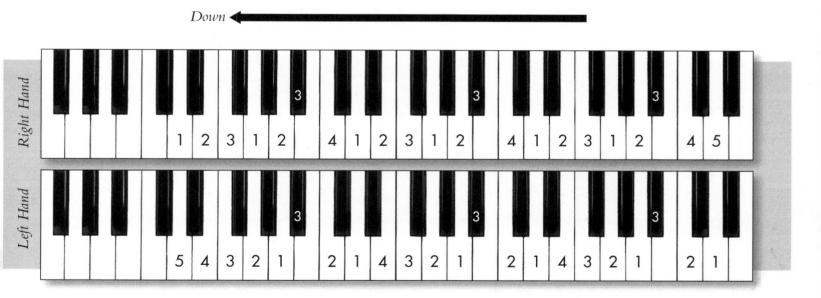

A MAJOR SCALE

Hands separately and together an octave apart in similar motion: 3 Octaves, up and down.

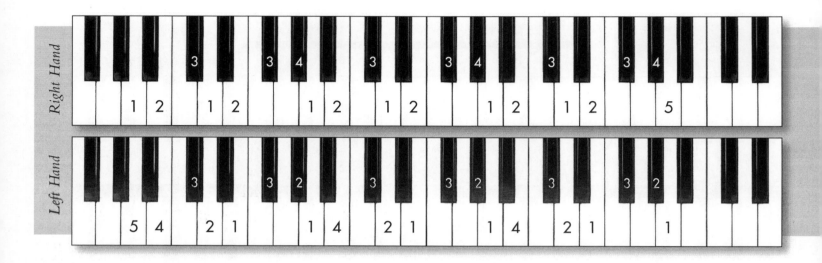

A MINOR HARMONIC SCALE

Hands separately and together an octave apart in similar motion: 3 Octaves, up and down.

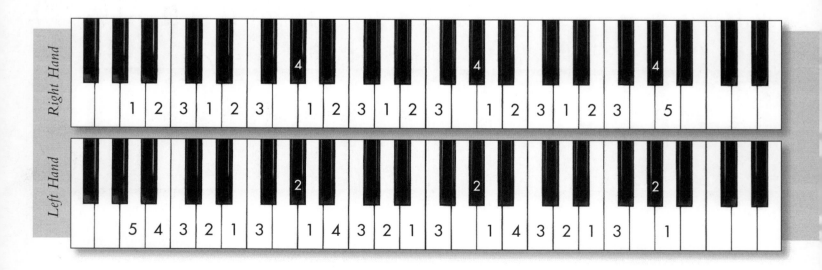

A MINOR MELODIC SCALE

Hands separately and together an octave apart in similar motion: 3 Octaves.

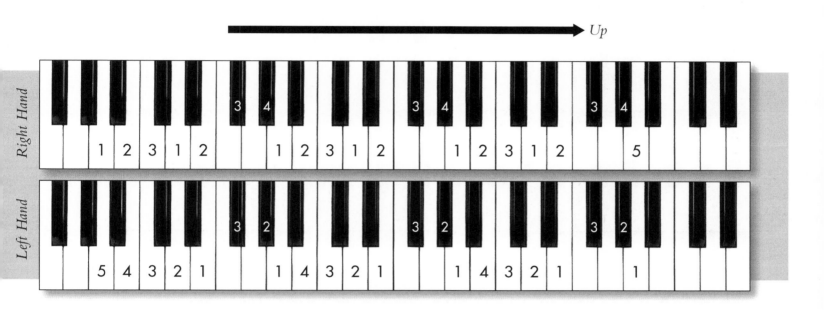

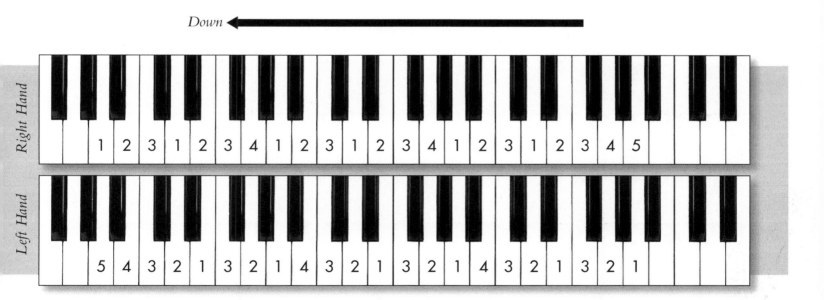

E MAJOR SCALE

Hands separately and together an octave apart in similar motion: 3 Octaves, up and down.

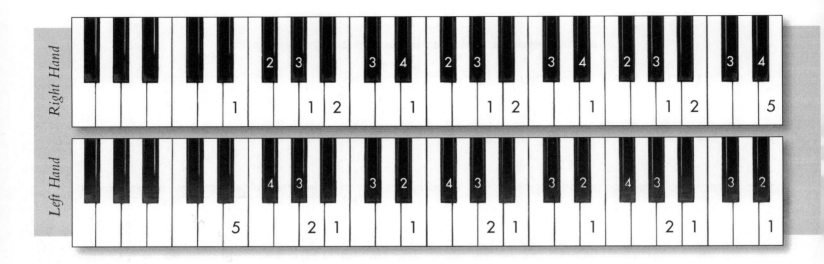

E MINOR HARMONIC SCALE

Hands separately and together an octave apart in similar motion: 3 Octaves, up and down.

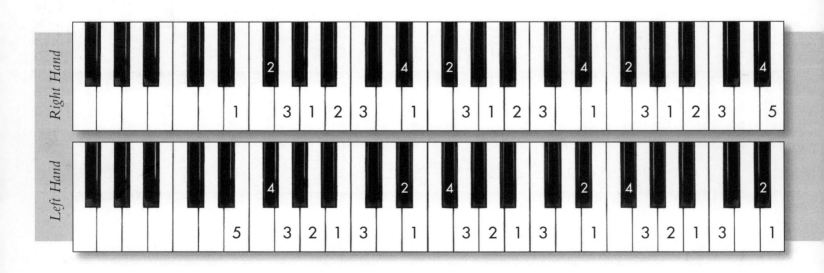

E MINOR MELODIC SCALE

Hands separately and together an octave apart in similar motion: 3 Octaves.

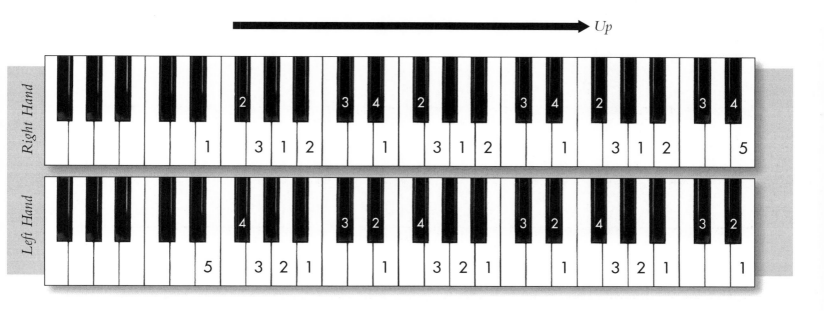

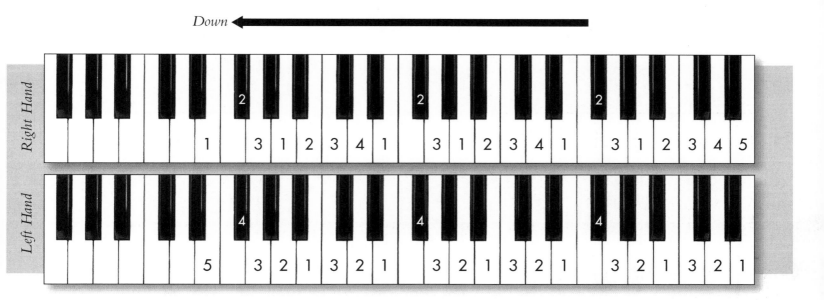

B MAJOR SCALE

Hands separately and together an octave apart in similar motion: 3 Octaves, up and down.

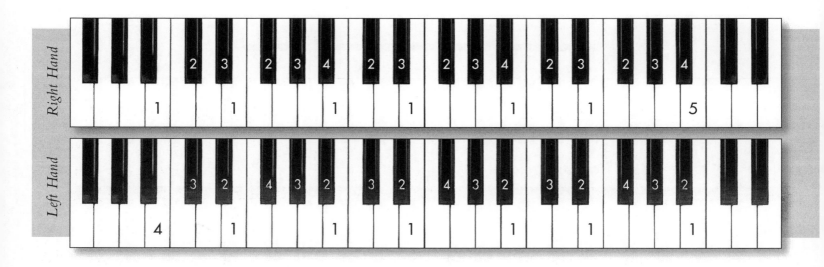

B MINOR HARMONIC SCALE

Hands separately and together an octave apart in similar motion: 3 Octaves, up and down.

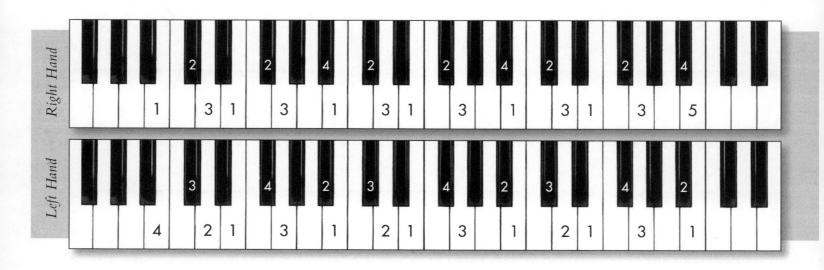

B MINOR MELODIC SCALE

Hands separately and together an octave apart in similar motion: 3 Octaves.

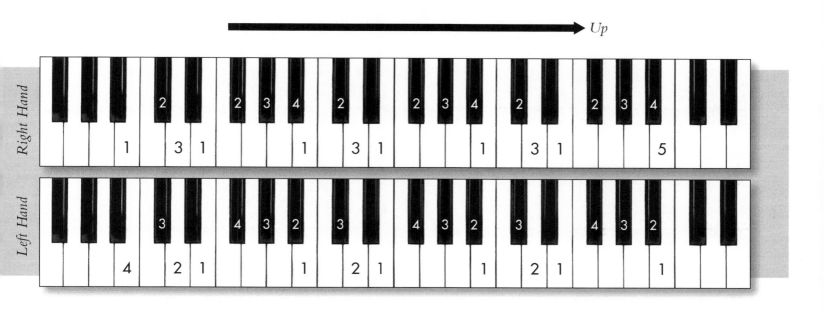

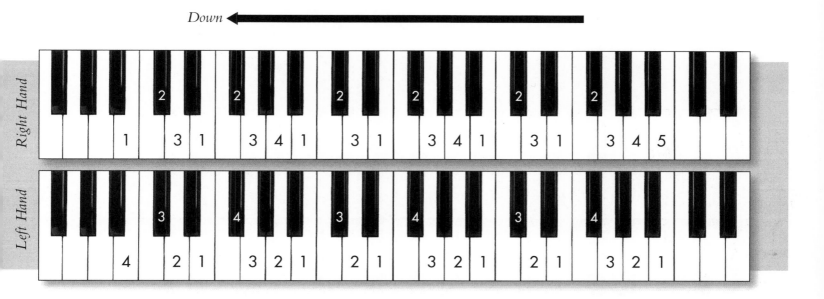

F♯ MAJOR SCALE

Hands separately and together an octave apart in similar motion: 3 Octaves, up and down.

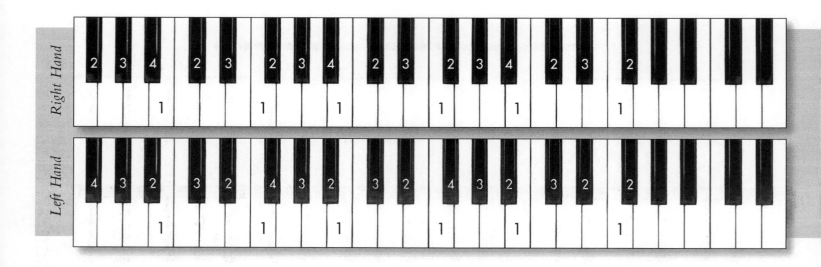

F♯ MINOR HARMONIC SCALE

Hands separately and together an octave apart in similar motion: 3 Octaves, up and down.

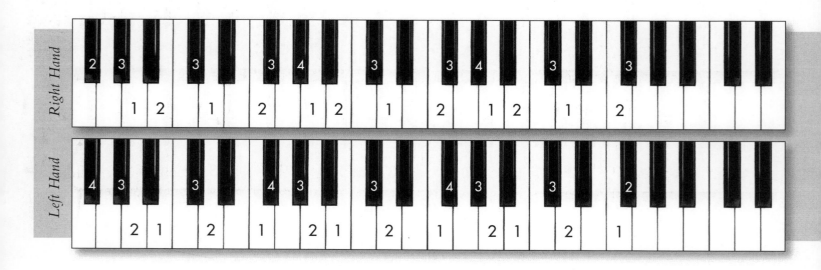

F♯ MINOR MELODIC SCALE

Hands separately and together an octave apart in similar motion: 3 Octaves.

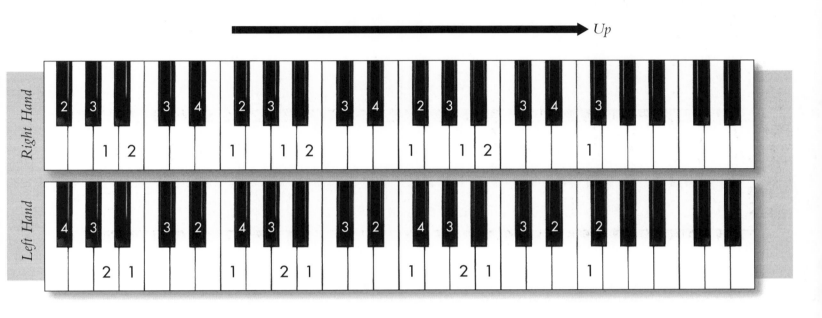

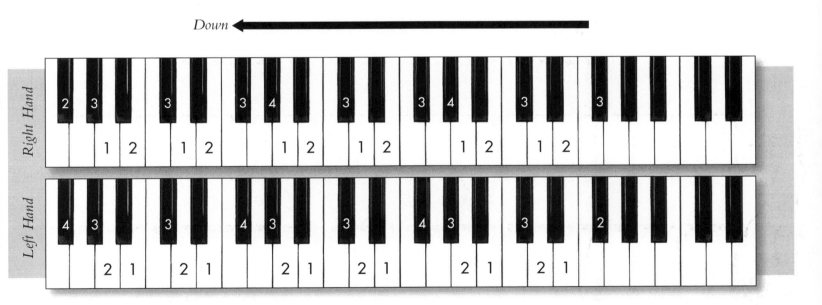

D♭ MAJOR SCALE

Hands separately and together an octave apart in similar motion: 3 Octaves, up and down.

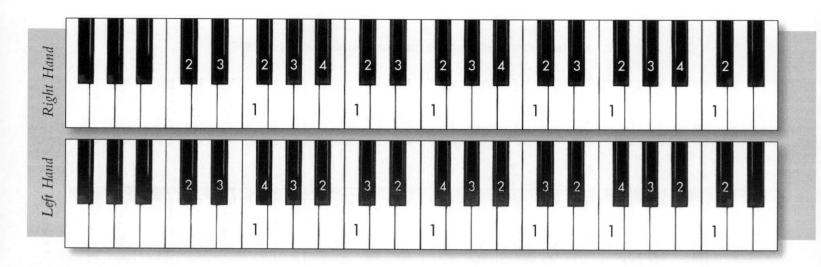

C♯ MINOR HARMONIC SCALE

Hands separately and together an octave apart in similar motion: 3 Octaves, up and down.

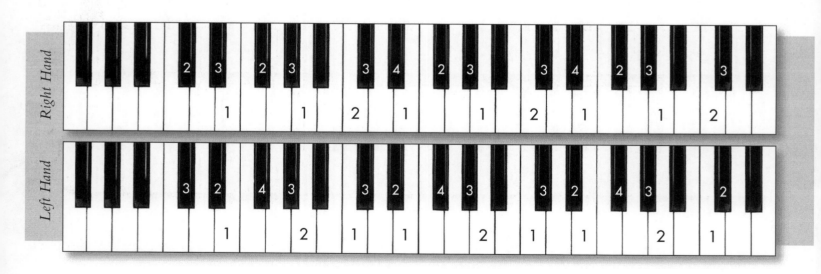

C♯ MINOR MELODIC SCALE

Hands separately and together an octave apart in similar motion: 3 Octaves.

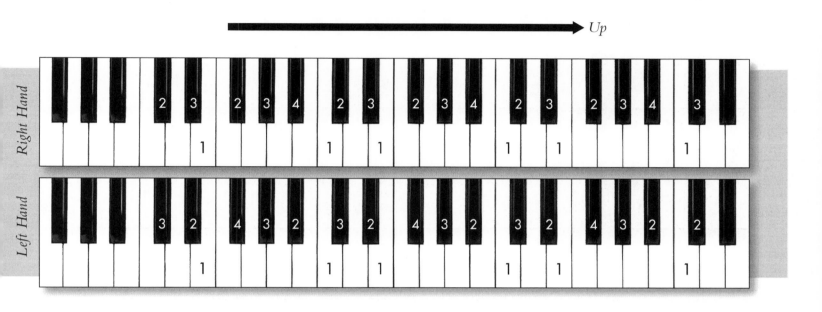

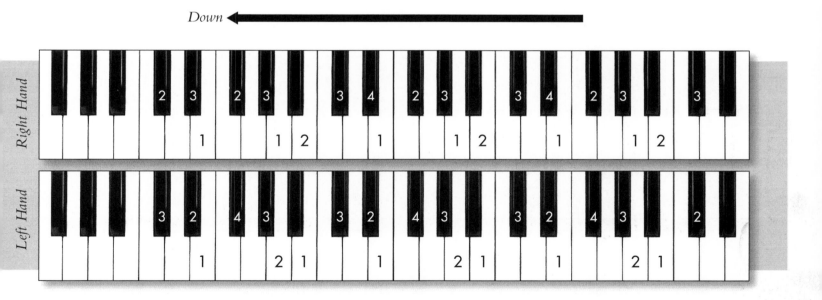

A♭ MAJOR SCALE

Hands separately and together an octave apart in similar motion: 3 Octaves, up and down.

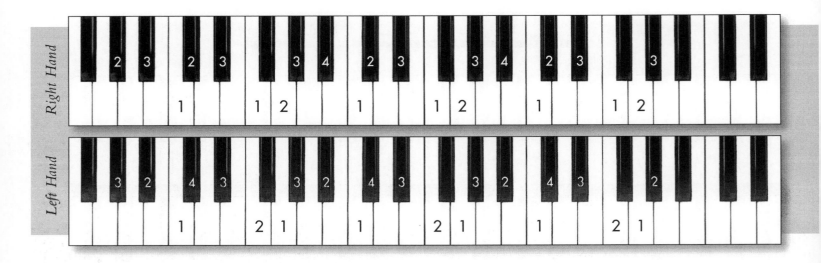

G♯ MINOR HARMONIC SCALE (enharmonic A♭)

Hands separately and together an octave apart in similar motion: 3 Octaves, up and down.

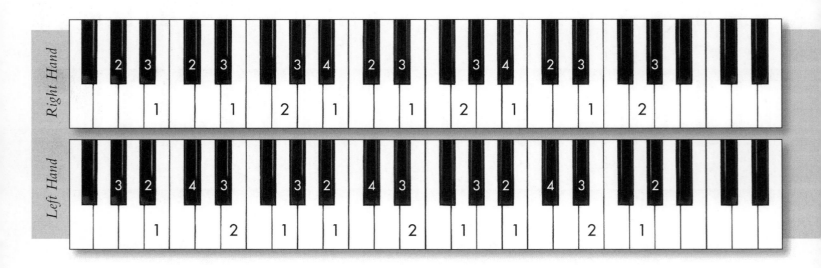

G# MINOR MELODIC SCALE (enharmonic A♭)

Hands separately and together an octave apart in similar motion: 3 Octaves.

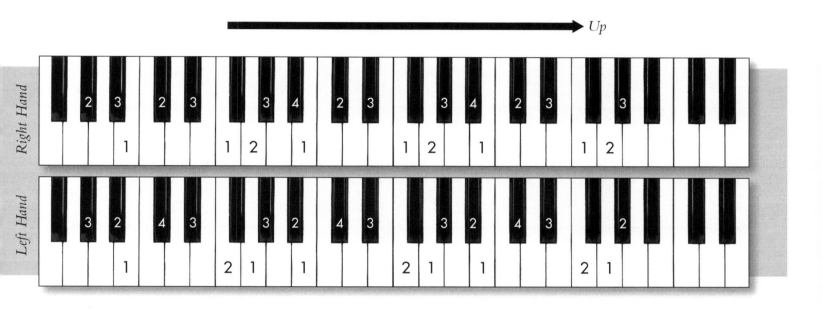

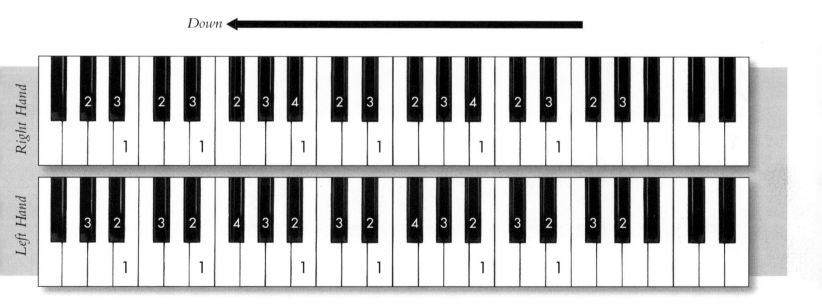

E♭ MAJOR SCALE

Hands separately and together an octave apart in similar motion: 3 Octaves, up and down.

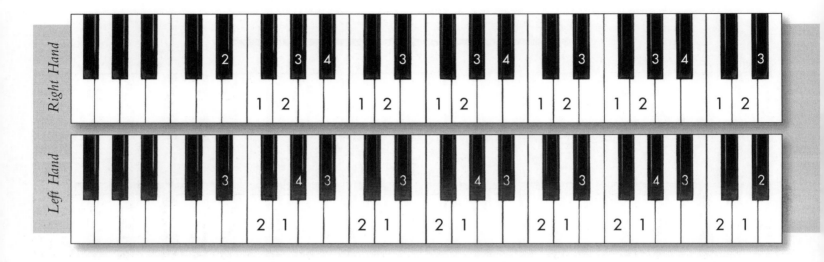

E♭ MINOR HARMONIC SCALE

Hands separately and together an octave apart in similar motion: 3 Octaves, up and down.

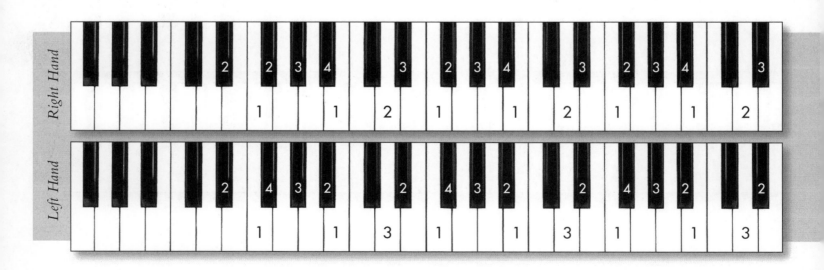

E♭ MINOR MELODIC SCALE

Hands separately and together an octave apart in similar motion: 3 Octaves.

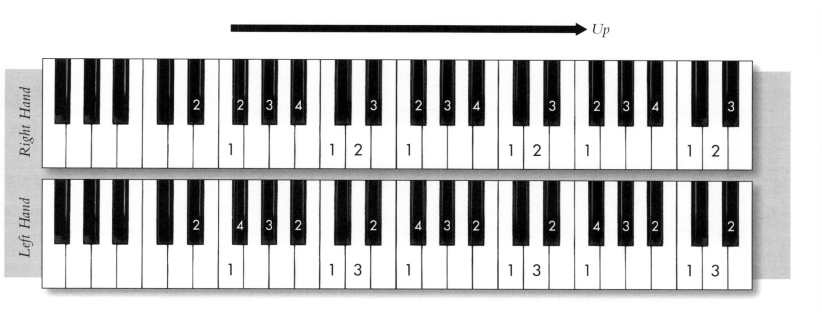

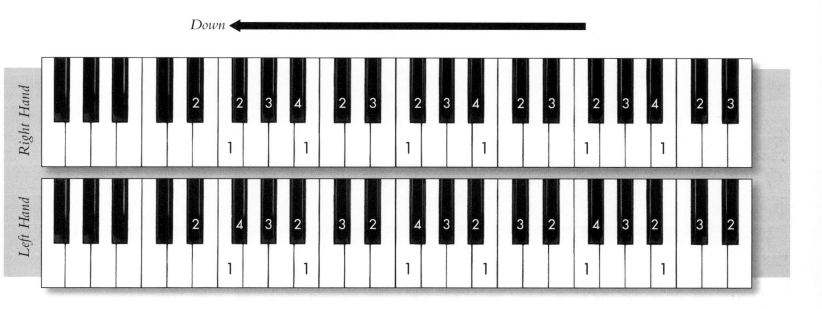

B♭ MAJOR SCALE

Hands separately and together an octave apart in similar motion: 3 Octaves, up and down.

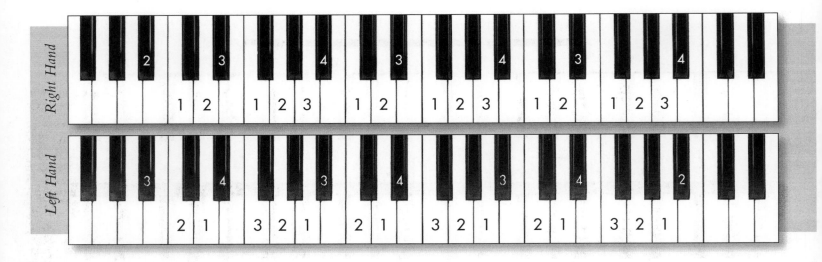

B♭ MINOR HARMONIC SCALE

Hands separately and together an octave apart in similar motion: 3 Octaves, up and down.

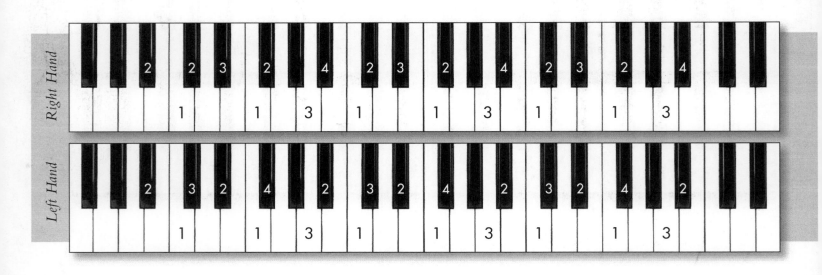

B♭ MINOR MELODIC SCALE

Hands separately and together an octave apart in similar motion: 3 Octaves.

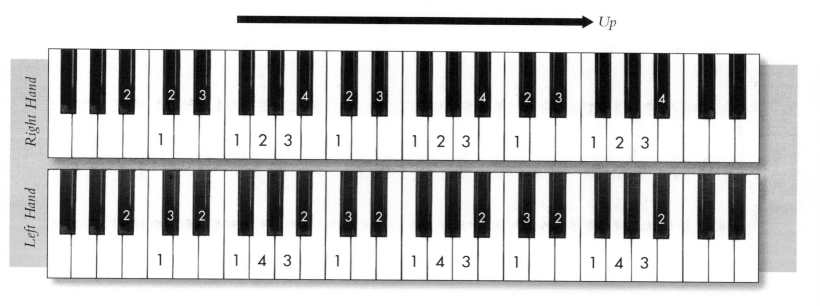

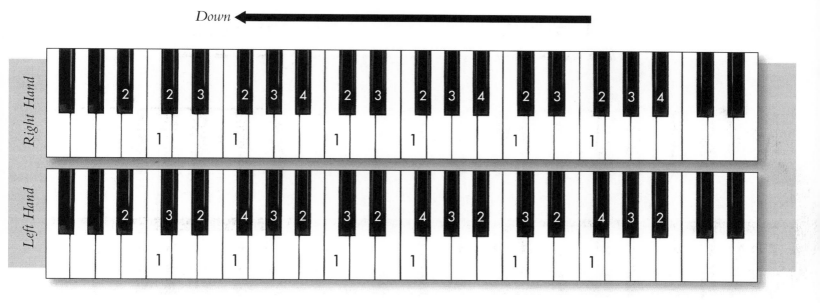

F MAJOR SCALE

Hands separately and together an octave apart in similar motion: 3 Octaves, up and down.

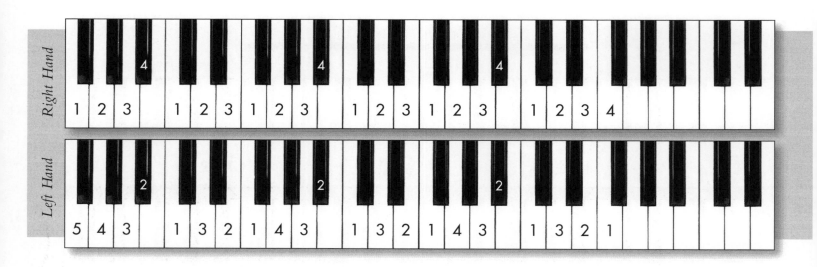

F MINOR HARMONIC SCALE

Hands separately and together an octave apart in similar motion: 3 Octaves, up and down.

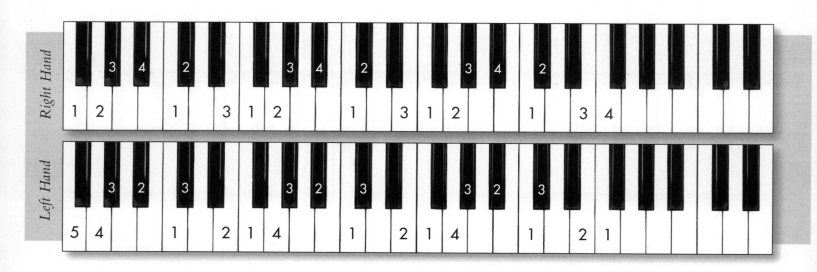

F MINOR MELODIC SCALE

Hands separately and together an octave apart in similar motion: 3 Octaves.

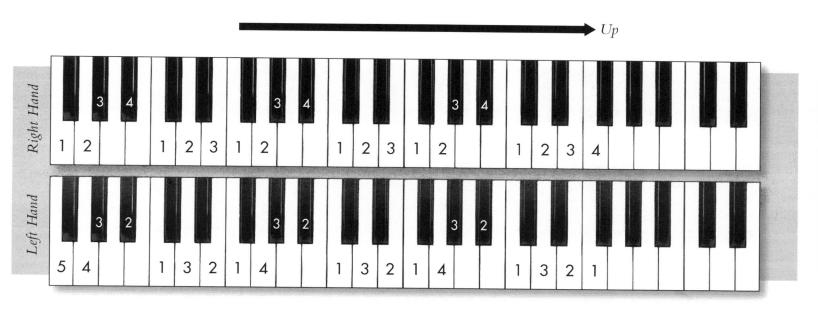

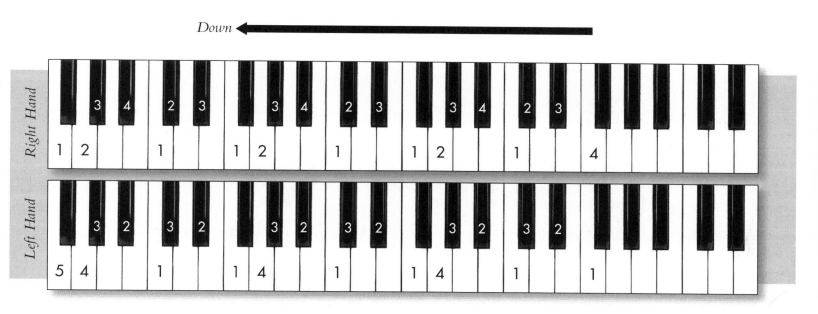

Candidates choose <u>either</u> Group 1 <u>or</u> Group 2

F MAJOR CONTRARY MOTION

Hands together beginning and ending on the key-note (unison): 2 Octaves, outwards and inwards.
Notes played together with both hands are shown using the same geometric shape.

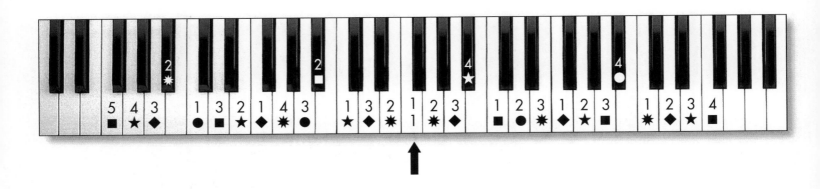

Db MAJOR CONTRARY MOTION (enharmonic C#)

Hands together beginning and ending on the key-note (unison): 2 Octaves, outwards and inwards.
Notes played together with both hands are shown using the same geometric shape.

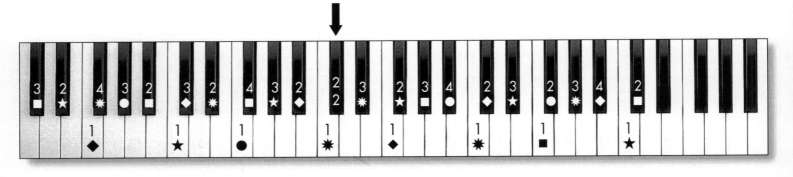

F MINOR CONTRARY MOTION

Hands together beginning and ending on the key-note (unison): 2 Octaves, outwards amd inwards.
Notes played together with both hands are shown using the same geometric shape.

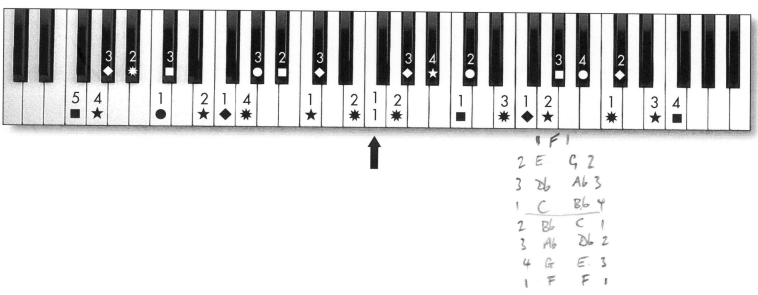

2	E	G	2
3	D♭	A♭	3
1	C	B♭	4
2	B♭	C	1
3	A♭	D♭	2
4	G	E	3
1	F	F	1

C# MINOR CONTRARY MOTION (enharmonic D♭)

Hands together beginning and ending on the key-note (unison): 2 Octaves, outwards and inwards.
Notes played together with both hands are shown using the same geometric shape.

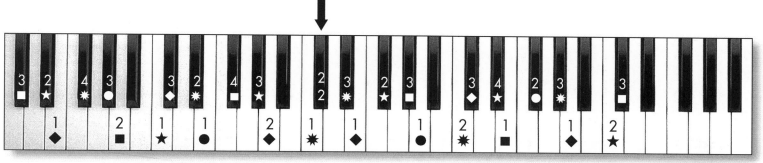

2	C#	2(3)	
1	B#	D#	3(4)
2	A	E	1
3	G#	F#	2
4	F#	G#	3
1	E	A	1
2	D#	B#	2
3	C#	C#	3

Candidates choose <u>either</u> Group 1 <u>or</u> Group 2

F♯ MAJOR CONTRARY MOTION (enharmonic G♭)

Hands together beginning and ending on the key-note (unison): 2 Octaves, outwards and inwards.
Notes played together with both hands are shown using the same geometric shape.

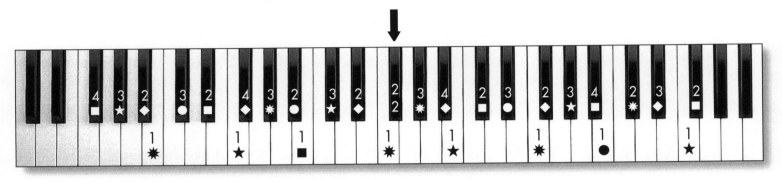

B♭ MAJOR CONTRARY MOTION

Hands together beginning and ending on the key-note (unison): 2 Octaves, outwards and inwards.
Notes played together with both hands are shown using the same geometric shape.

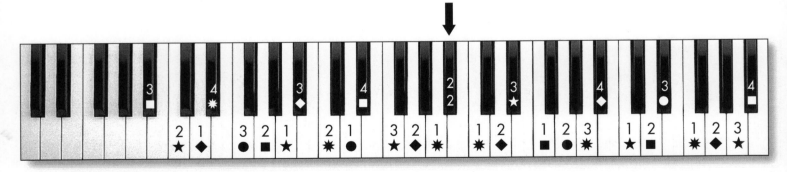

F♯ MINOR CONTRARY MOTION

Hands together beginning and ending on the key-note (unison): 2 Octaves, outwards and inwards.
Notes played together with both hands are shown using the same geometric shape.

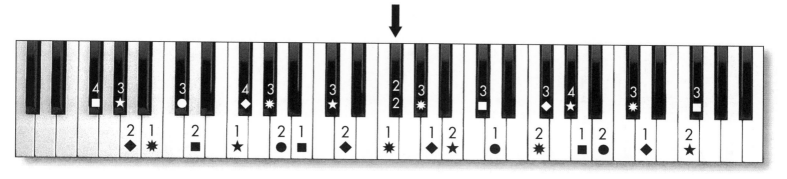

B♭ MINOR CONTRARY MOTION

Hands together beginning and ending on the key-note (unison): 2 Octaves, outwards and inwards.
Notes played together with both hands are shown using the same geometric shape.

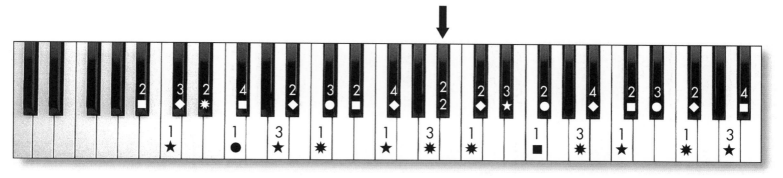

CHROMATIC SCALE STARTING ON C

Hands separately and together an octave apart: 3 Octaves, up and down.

♩ = 72 *(minimum speed recommended by the ABRSM)*

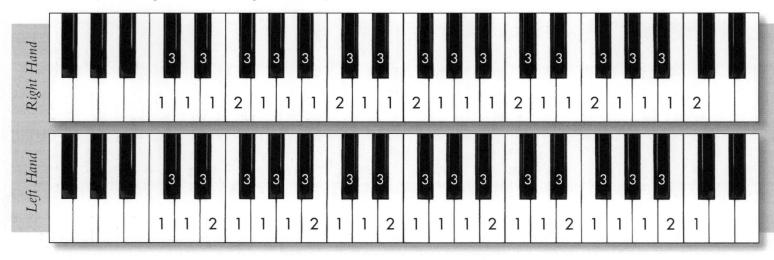

CHROMATIC SCALE STARTING ON C#/D♭

Hands separately and together an octave apart: 3 Octaves, up and down.

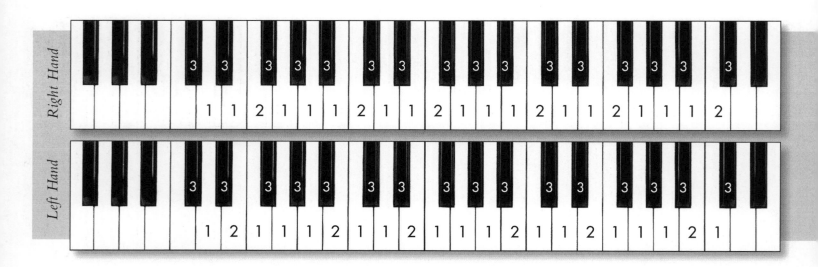

CHROMATIC SCALE STARTING ON D

Hands separately and together an octave apart: 3 Octaves, up and down.

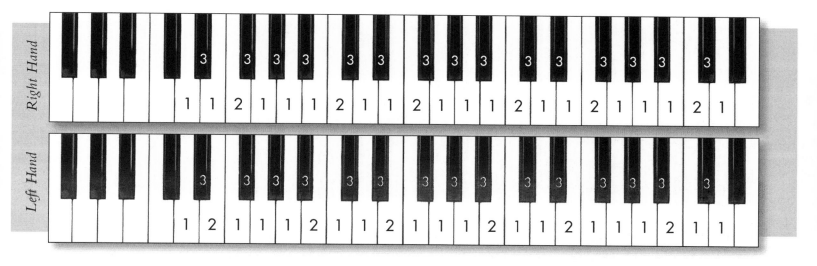

CHROMATIC SCALE STARTING ON D♯/E♭

Hands separately and together an octave apart: 3 Octaves, up and down.

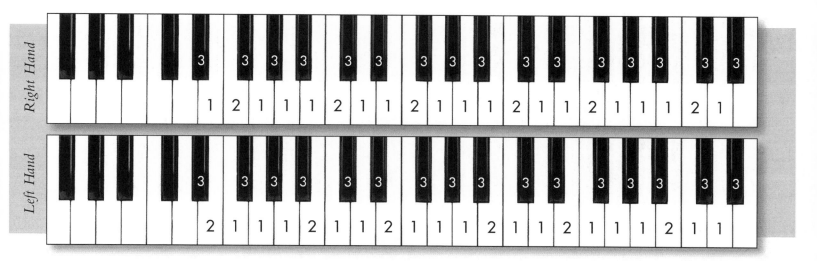

CHROMATIC SCALE STARTING ON E

Hands separately and together an octave apart: 3 Octaves, up and down.

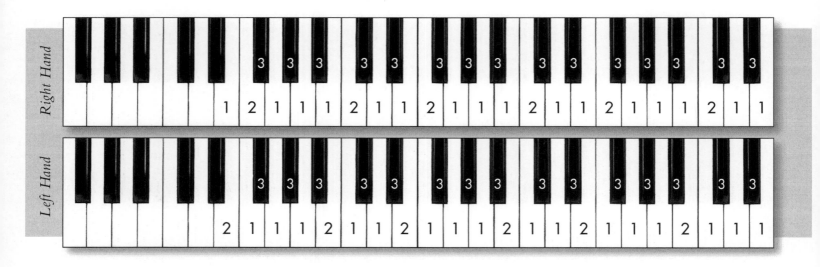

CHROMATIC SCALE STARTING ON F

Hands separately and together an octave apart: 3 Octaves, up and down.

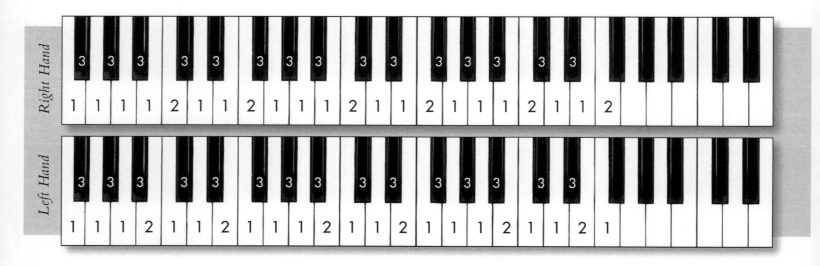

CHROMATIC SCALE STARTING ON F♯/G♭

Hands separately and together an octave apart: 3 Octaves, up and down.

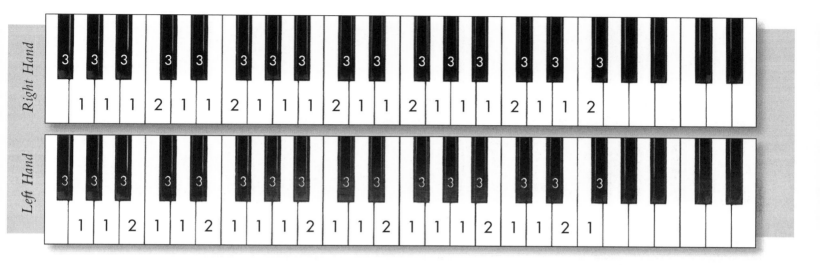

CHROMATIC SCALE STARTING ON G

Hands separately and together an octave apart: 3 Octaves, up and down.

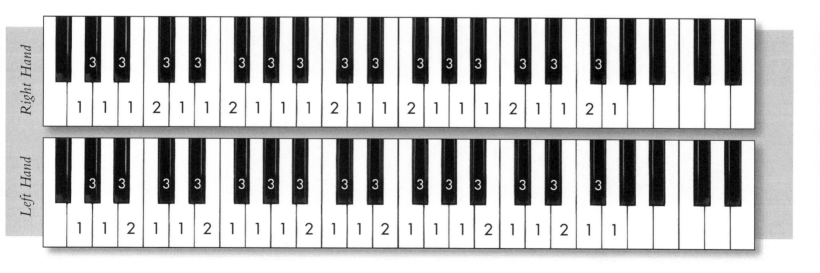

CHROMATIC SCALE STARTING ON G♯/A♭

Hands separately and together an octave apart: 3 Octaves, up and down.

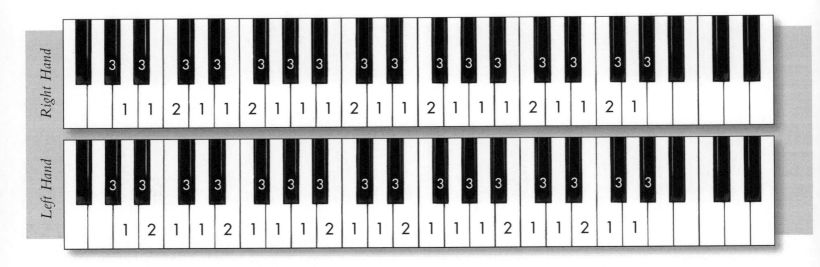

CHROMATIC SCALE STARTING ON A

Hands separately and together an octave apart: 3 Octaves, up and down.

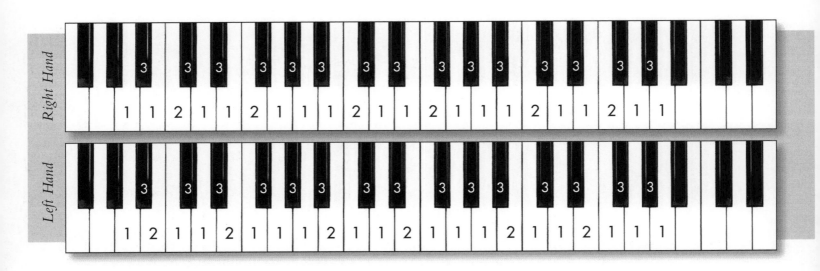

CHROMATIC SCALE STARTING ON A♯/B♭

Hands separately and together an octave apart: 3 Octaves, up and down.

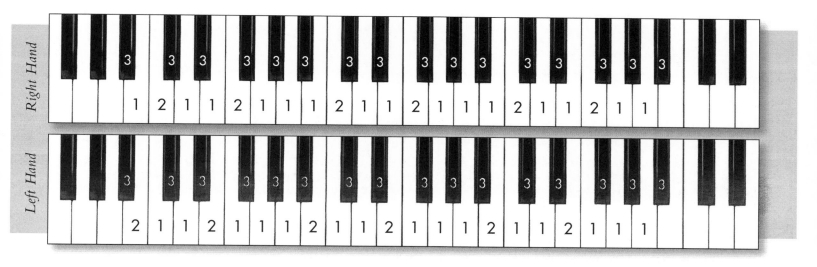

CHROMATIC SCALE STARTING ON B

Hands separately and together an octave apart: 3 Octaves, up and down.

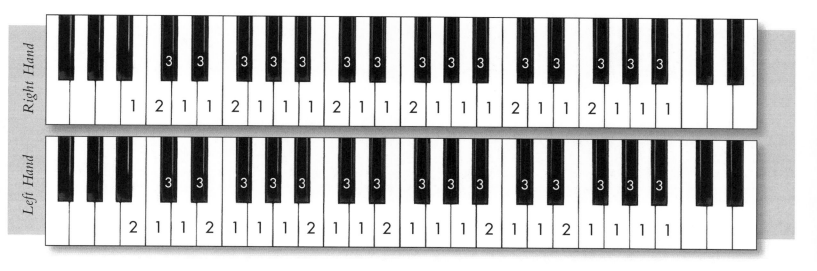

CHROMATIC SCALE IN CONTRARY MOTION
STARTING ON D

Hands together beginning and ending on the same note (unison): 2 Octaves, outwards and inwards.
Notes played together with both hands are shown using the same geometric shape.

♩ = 72 *(minimum speed recommended by the ABRSM)*

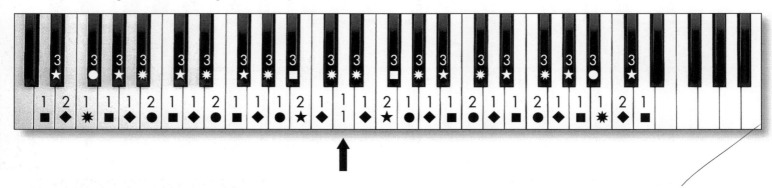

CHROMATIC SCALE IN CONTRARY MOTION
STARTING ON A♭

Hands together beginning and ending on the same note (unison): 2 Octaves, outwards amd inwards.
Notes played together with both hands are shown using the same geometric shape.

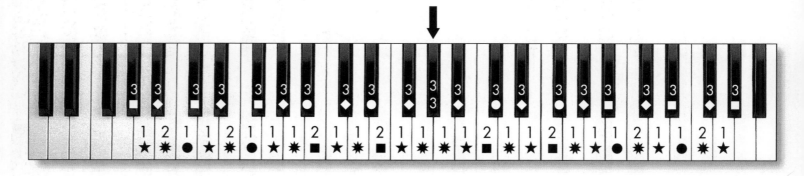

C MAJOR ARPEGGIO

Hands separately and together an octave apart: 3 Octaves, up and down.

♩ = 88 *(minimum speed recommended by the ABRSM)*

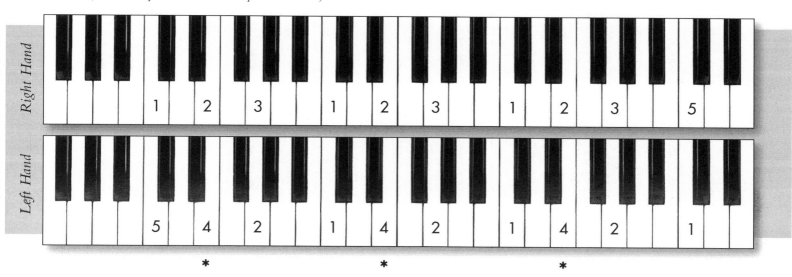

* alternative 3

C MINOR ARPEGGIO

Hands separately and together an octave apart: 3 Octaves, up and down.

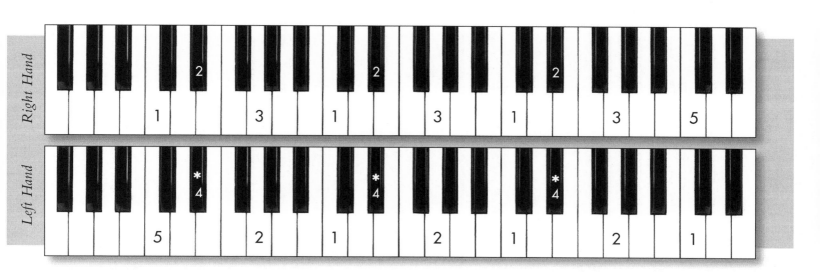

* alternative 3

N.B. The arpeggios are written without a time signature in groups of four quavers with the final note as a crotchet.

G MAJOR ARPEGGIO

Hands separately and together an octave apart: 3 Octaves, up and down.

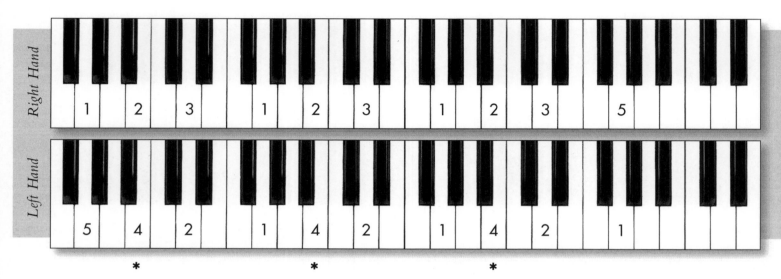

* alternative 3

G MINOR ARPEGGIO

Hands separately and together an octave apart: 3 Octaves, up and down.

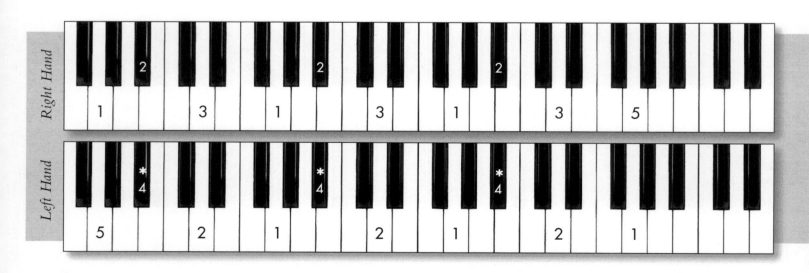

* alternative 3

D MAJOR ARPEGGIO

Hands separately and together an octave apart: 3 Octaves, up and down.

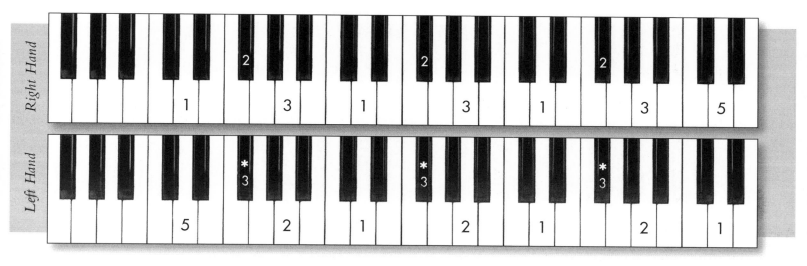

* alternative 4

D MINOR ARPEGGIO

Hands separately and together an octave apart: 3 Octaves, up and down.

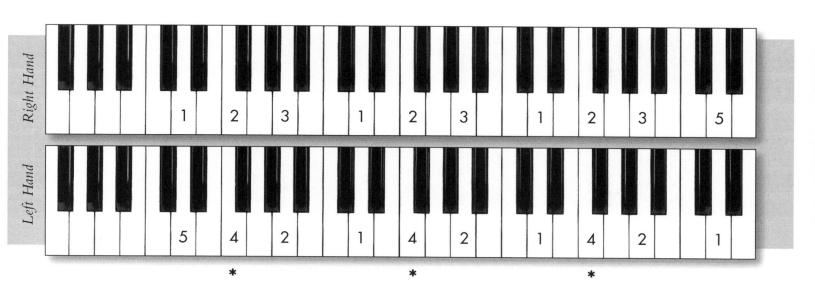

* alternative 3

A MAJOR ARPEGGIO

Hands separately and together an octave apart: 3 Octaves, up and down.

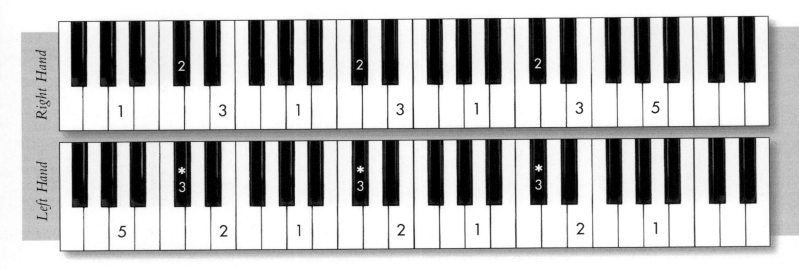

* alternative 4

A MINOR ARPEGGIO

Hands separately and together an octave apart: 3 Octaves, up and down.

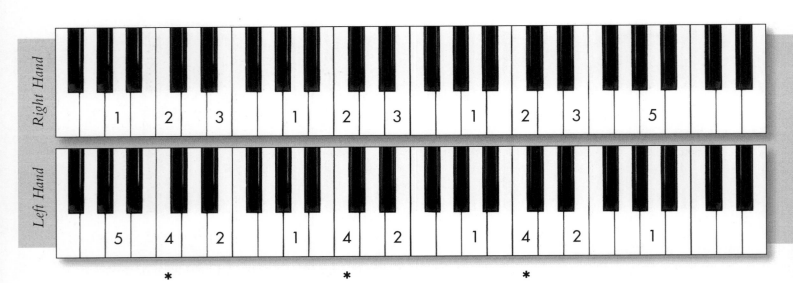

* alternative 3

E MAJOR ARPEGGIO

Hands separately and together an octave apart: 3 Octaves, up and down.

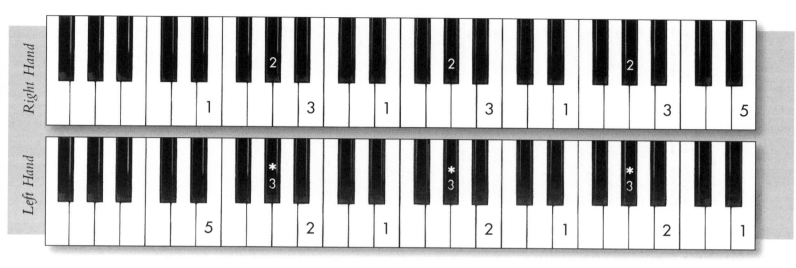

* alternative 4

E MINOR ARPEGGIO

Hands separately and together an octave apart: 3 Octaves, up and down.

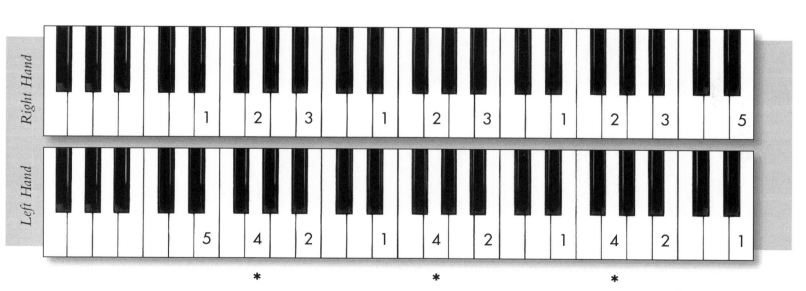

* alternative 3

B MAJOR ARPEGGIO

Hands separately and together an octave apart: 3 Octaves, up and down.

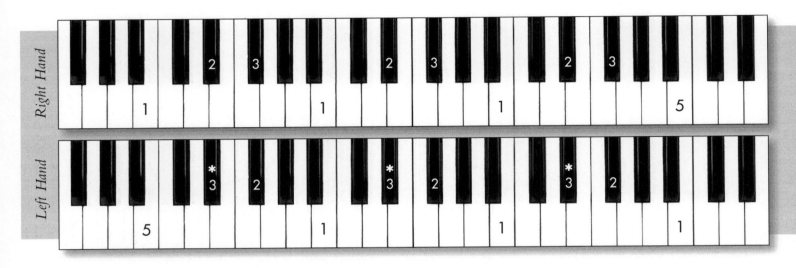

* alternative 4

B MINOR ARPEGGIO

Hands separately and together an octave apart: 3 Octaves, up and down.

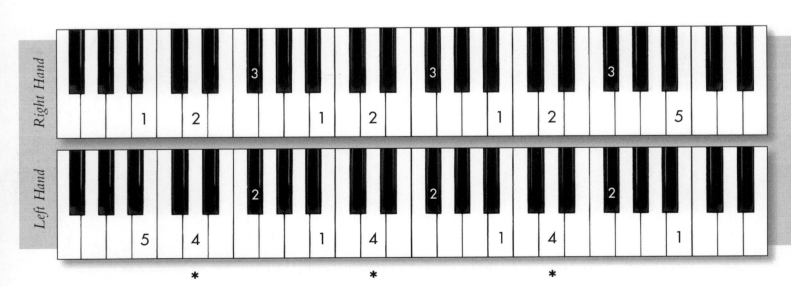

* alternative 3

F# MAJOR ARPEGGIO (enharmonic G♭)

Hands separately and together an octave apart: 3 Octaves, up and down.

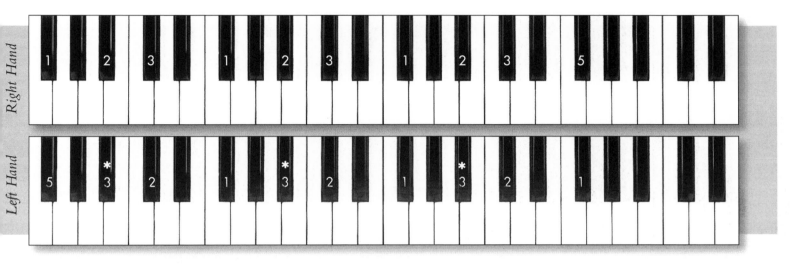

* alternative 4

F# MINOR ARPEGGIO

Hands separately and together an octave apart: 3 Octaves, up and down.

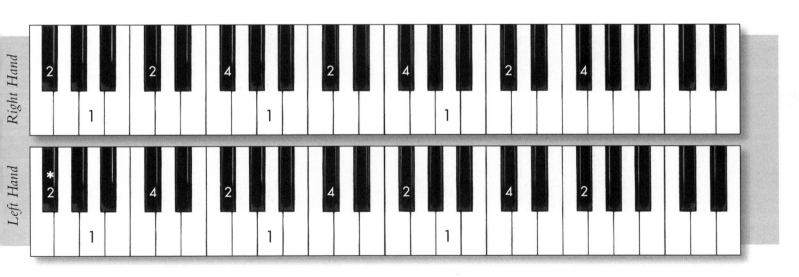

* alternative 3

D♭ MAJOR ARPEGGIO (enharmonic C♯)

Hands separately and together an octave apart: 3 Octaves, up and down.

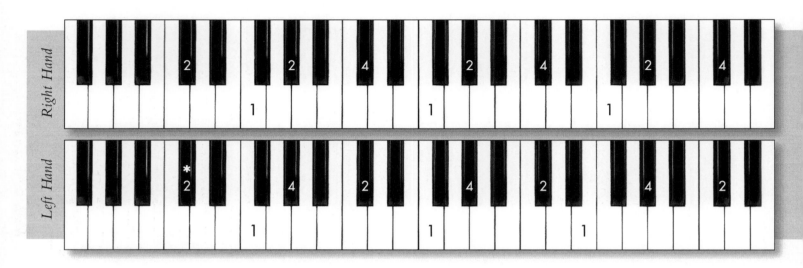

* alternative 3

C♯ MINOR ARPEGGIO (enharmonic D♭)

Hands separately and together an octave apart: 3 Octaves, up and down.

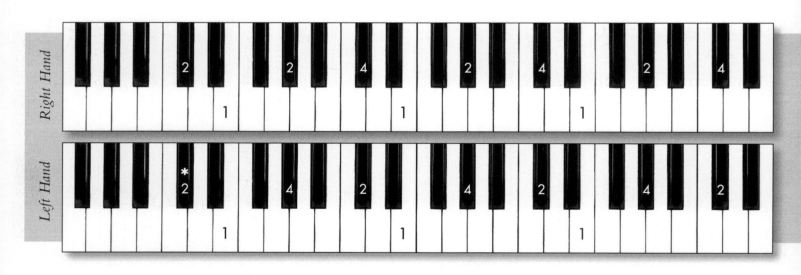

* alternative 3

A♭ MAJOR ARPEGGIO (enharmonic G♯)

Hands separately and together an octave apart: 3 Octaves, up and down.

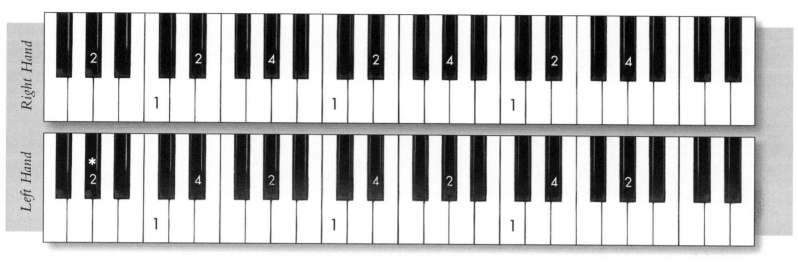

* alternative 3

G♯ MINOR ARPEGGIO (enharmonic A♭)

Hands separately and together an octave apart: 3 Octaves, up and down.

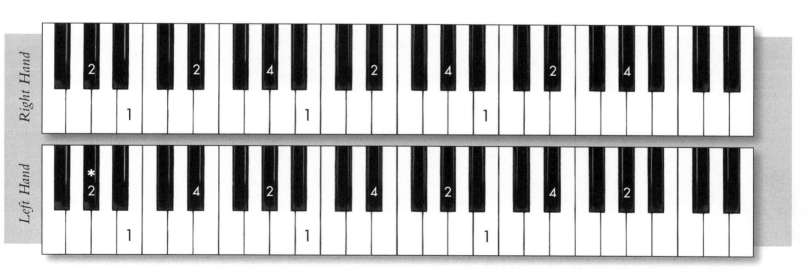

* alternative 3

E♭ MAJOR ARPEGGIO

Hands separately and together an octave apart: 3 Octaves, up and down.

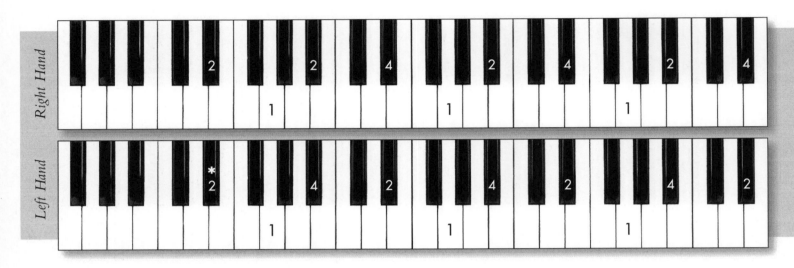

* alternative 3

E♭ MINOR ARPEGGIO

Hands separately and together an octave apart: 3 Octaves, up and down.

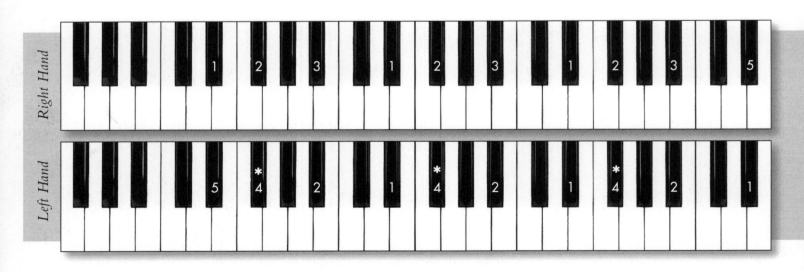

* alternative 3

B♭ MAJOR ARPEGGIO

Hands separately and together an octave apart: 3 Octaves, up and down.

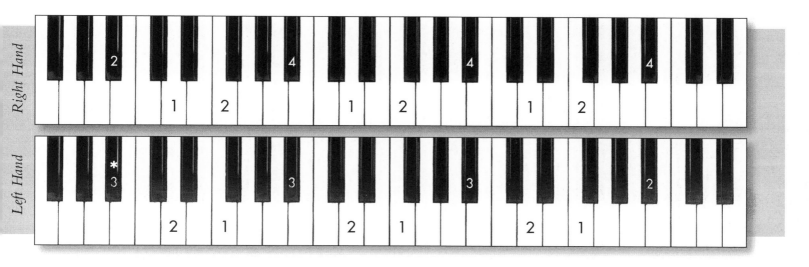

* alternative 4

B♭ MINOR ARPEGGIO

Hands separately and together an octave apart: 3 Octaves, up and down.

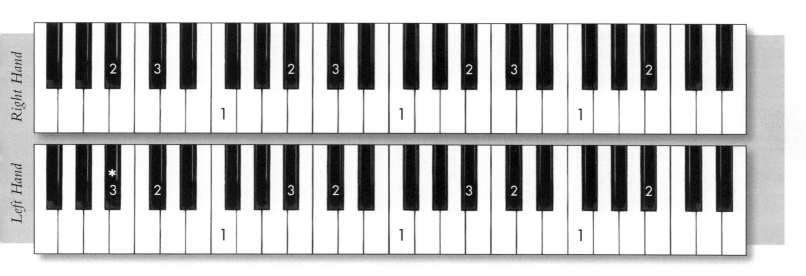

* alternative 4

Arpeggios

F MAJOR ARPEGGIO

Hands separately and together an octave apart: 3 Octaves, up and down.

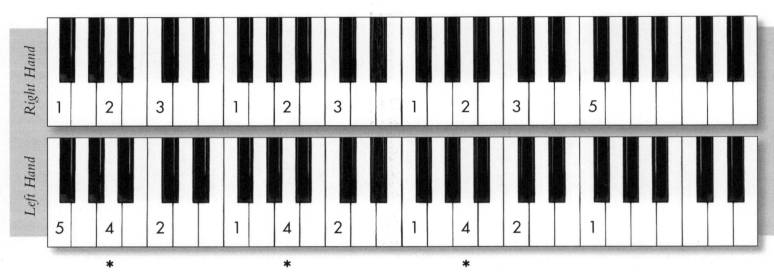

* alternative 3

F MINOR ARPEGGIO

Hands separately and together an octave apart: 3 Octaves, up and down.

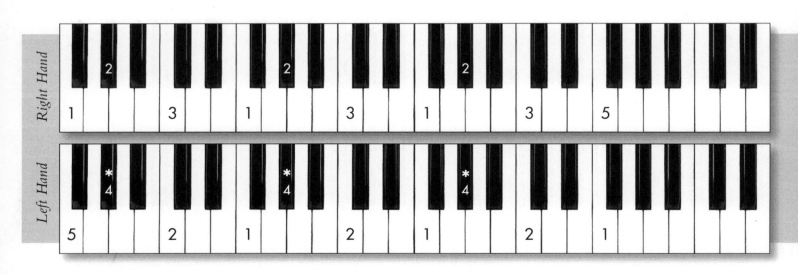

* alternative 3